God, is this Your Final Answer?

Bible Meditation and Journaling For Life

OTHER BOOKS BY Dr. M. DUANE RAWLINS

More than a Father

Raising Kids right in a World gone wrong

BOOKS PENDING

God, if this is Your final Answer,
How then should we live?

God, is this Your Final Answer?

Bible Meditation and Journaling For Life

Dr. M. Duane Rawlins

AMuzement Publications

Cover design by Brenda DiAntonis at: enetgroup.com

God, is this Your Final Answer? by Dr. M. Duane
Rawlins.
Copyright © 2001 M. Duane Rawlins.

Scriptures taken from the HOLY BIBLE, NEW INTERNA-
TIONAL VERSION. Copyright ©1973, 1978, 1984 International
Bible Society. Used by Permission of Zondervan Bible Publishers.

Dedication

This book is dedicated to my wonderful grandchildren. Who I trust will carry on the family tradition of being young men and women of the Word.

PREFACE

Twenty-one years ago, I was introduced to Bible meditation by Campbell McAlpine in Kona Hawaii, where he was teaching a class for Youth With A Mission.

My wife Betty caught the vision and purchased his audio tapes. I was profoundly moved by the immediate changes that took place in her life as she began meditating and journaling on a daily basis. I soon followed her into a deeper, more personal study of God's Word as it applied to my life. Now 63 completed journals and 21 years later, I am motivated to write this book to encourage you to spend quality time alone with God on a daily basis.

I have selected some of the most meaningful scriptures and concepts that have blessed my life and caused me to covenant with God to spend time alone with Him on a daily basis.

My great hope and earnest prayer is that you would be drawn to spending time alone with God and journaling what you are learning. So much of what you will get out of this time depends on your heart attitude as you enter in.

INTRODUCTION

I believe we have an urgent need for a time of solitude and daily study of God's Word. Since it is very difficult to meditate on God's Word when we are in the middle of conversation, noises, or distractions, I trust you will find a secret place where you can be alone.

Each section is undated so that you can go at your own pace and not feel guilty if you are not able to accomplish this on a daily basis. Once you have found a place of solitude, learn to sit in a relaxed way, in a restful, waiting, expectant mood. Allow the Holy Spirit to bring your mind and heart into focus on Him. This requires you to bring your thoughts obedient to Christ. It may be necessary to read a Psalm or scripture to quiet yourself before the Lord. As you get to the point where you are ready to receive from God, be sure you have separated yourself from all sin by asking God to cleanse your heart and forgive you of sins and impure thoughts. We need to wait on the Lord and expect daily cleaning. Finally, we need to submit ourselves to the Lordship of Jesus, asking Him to guide us and direct us in all that we do.

Next we begin reading the material we have chosen for the day. We need to read slowly word by word, pondering, considering, rereading, contemplating, and chewing on each thought. Ask the Holy Spirit to reveal what He wants you to know.

Webster's dictionary defines meditation as being engaged in thought or reflection, spiritual introspection. I would add to this, that the focus is on the Word of God and not any other form of meditation.

Here are some general questions to guide you to a deeper, more personal understanding of the text:

1. What is the main focus of the chapter or verse I am reading?

2. What is the historical, cultural or literary context in which it is presented?

3. What is it saying to me personally?

4. What should I do to conform my life to what is being taught here?

5. Does this bring up any experiences or situations that I need to correct or amend?

FOUNDATION MATERIAL

I have always been of the opinion that a teacher has not taught until the student has learned. Information can be brilliantly presented but it does not become learned until the student has understood and absorbed it into his own heart and mind.

The Judeo-Christian values, which once formed the foundations of our country's moral and ethical lifestyle, are now virtually non-existent. In times past converts came into church life with a basic understanding of right from wrong. This is no longer the case. We have no infrastructure based on the Word of God. The objective of this book is to assist you to get the principles from the word of God deeply imbedded in your heart.

For much of my life I have been a student of the Bible. I have also been an educator and have been very involved in teaching and training people. But the real truth of the matter is that for most of my earlier life I read the Bible trying to find *truth* to teach to someone else. For me it has been very exciting these last 21 years to be reading the Bible and hearing God speak directly to me through meditating on His Word.

DIFFERING BACKGROUNDS

Each one of you comes to God's Word with your own "unique" experiences. Some of you may have been raised in Christian homes; others may not know anything about a religious upbringing. Some of you may have been deeply involved in sin, drugs, or alcohol. Perhaps you are married or you have gone through a divorce or are still single. Perhaps you feel that there isn't anyone who knows you or understands you or your feelings. Perhaps you have suffered rejection as part of your upbringing. Whatever your background, the important thing to know and remember is that no one knows you like God the Father, God the Son, and God the Holy Spirit.

So many times, in our search for wholeness and to find a real purpose in life, we often misunderstand just what Christianity is all about. In this devotional book, I would like to help you to come to the realization that you are created for fellowship with God the Father, God the Son, and God the Holy Spirit.

Now, as well as through the ages, God loves each and every one of us as the individuals that we are. It is because of this love for us that He is desperately trying to get our attention. He wants so much to equip us, to instruct us, to warn us of dangers, and to assist us in becoming the person we are created to be. Like a loving human father, God wants only the best for us.

What would you like God to help you change about your life? What do you believe is your central purpose in life? How has God tried to get your attention as you have moved toward your goal? What kind of relationship did you have with your earthly father?

_____

_____

_____

_____

_____

_____

_____

_____

_____

_____

_____

_____

_____

_____

_____

_____

_____

_____

_____

WE ALL HAVE THE
SAME BEGINNING

No matter what our background, no matter what our training, no matter what our experience in life, we all started out as sinners and are separated from God's presence. In Romans 3:23, Paul reminds us that we have all sinned and fallen short of the Glory of God and there is only one way back into His fellowship and that's through Jesus. In Act 4:12 it clearly states, "Salvation is found in no one else, for there is no other name under heaven given to men by which we must be saved."

First John 4:9, further emphasizes this by stating, "This is how God showed His love among us: He sent His one and only Son into the world that we might live through Him."

What was your salvation experience like? How settled in your heart are you that you are saved? To what extent is Jesus Lord of your life?

GOD HAS NO GRANDCHILDREN

If we have been raised by godly parents or grand-parents we may tend to worship their God and thereby not make God *our* Father. As you read through this book, it will become more and more evident to you that there is no such thing as God having a *grandchild*. It is not the faith of our parents, the faith of our pastor, or the faith of our friends, but it is our own personal relationship with God that counts. It is you accepting Him as your personal Savior that puts you into a right relationship with the Father through His Son. It is not possible for one to become a close friend to someone, unless we put forth an effort to draw close to that person and get to know his or her likes and dislikes.

Jeremiah 9:23-24 says, "Let not the wise man boast of his wisdom or the strong man boast of his strength or the rich man boast of his riches, but let him who boasts boast about this: that he understands and knows me, that I am the LORD, who exercises kindness, justice and righteousness on earth, for in these I delight," declares the Lord.

Bible meditation brings us into a special place, a quiet place, a serene place, a place where we are able to get to really know Him. But let me add a caution: with every truth there comes a counterfeit. Today many are frightened by the word "meditation" because there are so many false forms of it. As you continue through this book, you will begin to see that true Bible mediation is centered on God's Word and does not have anything to do with other kinds of meditation.

Questions to ponder: How often have you looked to others to help build your faith rather than having a personal relationship with God? What things are you most often likely to boast about when talking to friends? How fully do you understand the importance of Bible meditation?

_____

_____

_____

_____

_____

_____

_____

_____

_____

_____

_____

_____

_____

WHAT IS YOUR AMBITION IN LIFE?

Many of us go through phases where we try to decide for ourselves what is really important. Some seek fame or fortune. Others want desperately to be successful at any cost. Still others are merely interested in finding happiness. The truth of the matter is this: "Love the Lord your God with all your heart and with all your soul and with all your mind and with all your strength" (Mark 12:30).

I have found that happiness isn't something you seek but it is a result of being in the right relationship with God. True success comes from you being the person that God created you to be and by doing the things that He wants you to accomplish. This may or may not bring fame or fortune, but it certainly will provide you with the opportunity to seek out that which is most important to you.

If we truly want to please God, we will pay close attention to 2 Cor. 5:9 where Paul indicates that our ambition should be just that, to please God. Also in Col. 1:9,10 we discover what the pay off is for pleasing God. One of the primary ways this can be accomplished is to spend time alone, in God's Word. This will lead to developing a close relationship with the Living God and "falling in love" with the Creator of the universe.

How often have you reexamined at your life to see what your ambitions are? Where does the search for wisdom fit into your priorities in life? What is your relationship with God like? How much of your life is an expression of God's will?

_____

_____

_____

_____

_____

_____

_____

_____

_____

_____

_____

_____

_____

_____

_____

_____

_____

_____

_____

_____

WHAT IS YOUR CONCEPT OF GOD?

For years I traveled under some false concepts of
what God was like. Due to a conservative Christian background, I viewed God as being harsh,
judgmental, and only interested in *catching me* in
some sort of sin. My whole idea of what God was
really like was far too small. I would dare say the
same is true of your concept of God too, but this
can be remedied by spending time alone with Him
and experiencing the great love God has for each
of us. This requires a real commitment to spend
time in the Word. It requires discipline, diligence,
and sacrifice. If we are truly to know God, we
must learn His likes, His dislikes, His joy and His
sorrow.

Do you know what delights God? Do you know
what brings Him joy? Do you understand what
He hates and what things are an abomination to
Him? In Deuteronomy 30:11-20, Moses gives some
of his last counsel to the Israelites. Most is still
applicable to us today. He reminds them that "the
Word is very near you; it is in your mouth and in
your heart so you may obey it. See, I set before
you today life and prosperity, death and destruc-
tion. For I command you today to love the LORD
your God, to walk in His ways, and to keep His

commands, decrees and laws; then you will live and increase, and the LORD your God will bless you in the land you are entering to possess."

The same thing is true today. We need to be ready and willing to obey God's Word.. Bible meditation is the very discipline that will revolutionize your life when it becomes a continued part of your devotions. Paul instructs Timothy, "Be diligent in these matters; give yourself wholly to them, so that everyone may see your progress" (1 Tim. 4:15). And Jesus reminded his disciples, "If you love me, you will obey what I command" (John 14:15). The best way to get acquainted with what He commands is to *daily* spend time in the Word.

How big is your God? Is there any problem in your life that He can't handle? Is God always good? What troubles have you faced that might cause you to question His goodness? What does the Bible say about His goodness?

_____

_____

_____

_____

_____

_____

_____

_____

_____

_____

WE ARE ALL SPIRITUAL BABIES

When we are born into the kingdom of God, we are immediately and supernaturally "new babes" in Christ. As with all babies, we are fragile, irresponsible, helpless, dependent, milk-drinking infants. We lack discernment and strength. When we start our Christian walk as babies, we stumble, we fall, and we make mistakes. But if we are fed, loved, and encouraged, we begin to grow. This nourishment must be spiritual food and the only source of this *food* is the Word of God. In 1 Corinthians 3:2, Paul reminds the Christians in Corinth, "I gave you milk, not solid food, for you were not yet ready for it. Indeed, you are still not ready."

In all of us there is a need to grow and develop and no longer be babies, but to mature first into adolescence and then to full adulthood. Just as little children need constant food, exercise, and sleep, growing Christians need to spend time in the Word exercising their minds and their spirits, drinking in the wisdom and truth that is in the Word of God.

What are some of the ways that you have promoted spiritual growth in your life? Which specific activity has caused the most spiritual growth?

SIGNS OF MATURITY

As we mature, we must learn to act on what we are reading in God's Word. In the process, we begin to put into practice the knowledge and understanding we have gained and *do* what is required of us according to God's Word. It is extremely vital that we not be simply exposed to Bible truths, but that we also allow them to come into our hearts. We must meditate on them and take them into our inner beings and let them pervade our thoughts and our attitudes. It is then that our character will begin to be formed.

There is no such thing as instant maturity any more than there is instant adulthood for a baby. Christian growth comes through hard-core gutsy perseverance to apply what you hear and obey it.

What are some of the signs of maturity evidenced in your life? What are some areas you feel you still need to grow in? Looking back over the last year which one of your character qualities has shown the most improve-ment? Select an area you would like to meditate on and improve in.

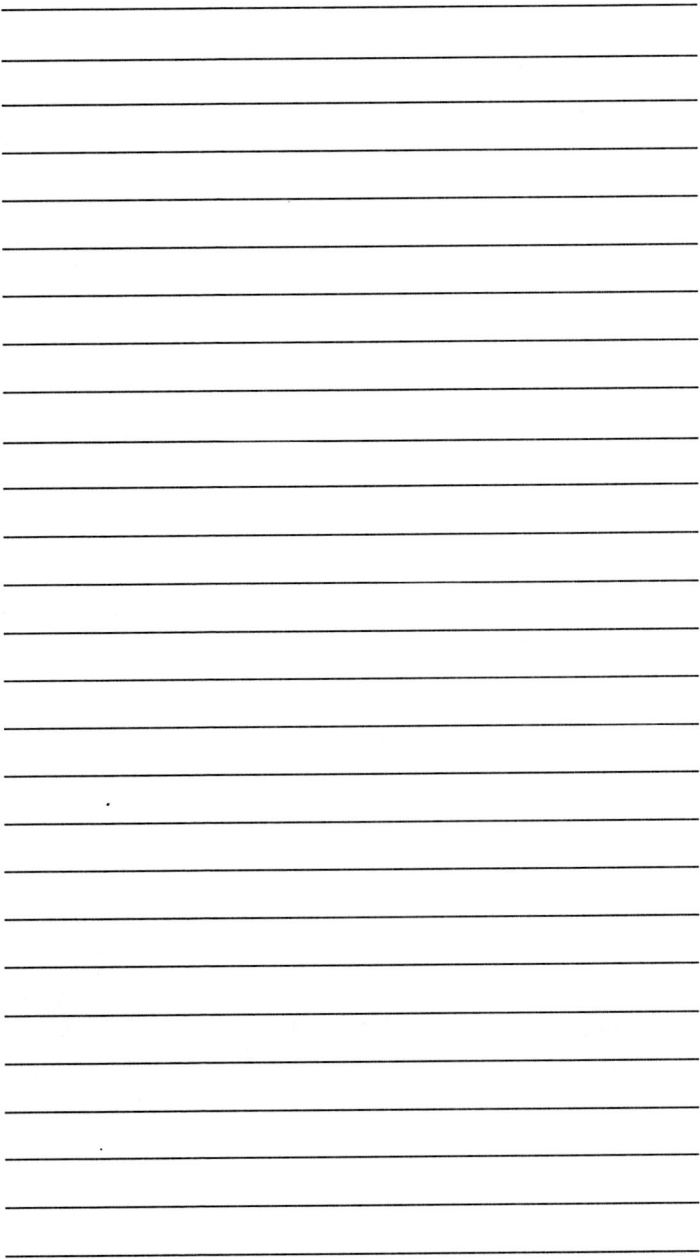

A PREREQUISITE FOR
BIBLE MEDITATION

If we want to be true meditators on the Word, it is absolutely essential that we believe that the Bible is from God. This holy book is comprised of sixty-six books and written over a period of 1,500 years with forty different authors. Remember there were no telephones, radios, television, or any other means for those authors to communicate other than being "divinely inspired" by the Holy Spirit. Several scriptures will help validate this for you. The first is found in 2 Timothy 3:16,17: "All Scripture is God-breathed and is useful for teaching, rebuking, correcting and training in righteousness, so that the man of God may be thoroughly equipped for every good work."

Another is 1 Peter 1:25, which states that "the word of the Lord stands forever." We are also reminded in Psalms 119:105 that "Your word is a lamp to my feet and a light for my path" and in Psalms119:89 that "Your word, O LORD, is eternal; it stands firm in the heavens." And Revelation 19:9 is infinitely clear: "These are the true words of God."

These scriptures underscore the authenticity of the Word, but perhaps the most important is that Jesus himself was identified as "The Word became flesh and made his dwelling among us" (John 1:14).

Select one of the scriptures above and commit it to memory. What can you do to enhance your belief that the Bible is the inspired Word of God?

_____

_____

_____

_____

_____

_____

_____

_____

_____

_____

_____

_____

_____

_____

_____

_____

_____

_____

_____

_____

_____

_____

_____

THE BOOK OF LIFE

Along with believing the Word of God to be directly breathed by God, we must also have faith that God is all wise, is truly our Creator and therefore, knows and understands everything about us. Deuteronomy 4:39 states clearly, "Acknowledge and take to heart this day that the LORD is God in heaven above and on the earth below. There is no other."

There are many scriptures that remind us, but one I particularly like is in Isaiah 48:17: "I am the LORD your God, who teaches you what is best for you, who directs you in the way you should go." The Bible reveals and glorifies God. It is the Book of Life. It is the Living Word of a Living God.

God himself reminds us in Matthew 24:35, "Heaven and earth will pass away, but my words will never pass away." If we truly want to be happy and successful, we must come to know God's Word, not only *that* He has spoken but also exactly *what* He has spoken. As our knowledge of God's Word grows we can be assured of what God's will is for our life. Many people are constantly frustrated because they feel they really never know God's will for their lives. Yet very little of their time is spent reading God's Word and trying to understand His plans and purpose for us. We need to look at the way He dealt with people in the past, what lies ahead in the future, and discern what we can expect.

In your life can you identify some of the thoughts God has spoken or quickened to you from His Word? In what ways are you challenged in attempting to know God's will for your life? How have you found help for personal problems while meditating on His Word?

_____

_____

_____

_____

_____

_____

_____

_____

_____

_____

_____

_____

_____

_____

_____

_____

_____

_____

DO YOU FIND THE
WORD OF GOD BORING?

Perhaps as you studied the Bible in the past you actually have been bored rather than inspired. Part of this may be due to a heart attitude, but understanding what you are reading is also a large part of your appreciation for what you have read. This is where it is important to read from a modern translation in which you can clearly understand what the Holy Spirit is saying. At the same time we must realize that while the Bible was written for *all* mankind, it also is directly applicable to each and every one of us individually. What we read is not meant for us to *apply* to others or just to *teach* others but was written to provide us individually with revelation. It is actually a daily confrontation with the Living God. And if we are not willing to put forth some effort to sit down and be confronted daily, most of us will experience little change in our lives.

But on the other hand, if we do put forth this effort and listen to the Word of God speak to us, we will learn how sin breaks the heart of the Father who loves us so deeply. Then we will want to stop our sinning. We will want to because we don't want to cause anymore hurt to Him who has such a real love for each one of us.

How has reading from a modern Bible translation increased your understanding of what you are reading? Describe an incident that expanded your understanding of the Word of God? Which books of the Bible have you avoided because they seemed boring or hard to understand?

_____

_____

_____

_____

_____

_____

_____

_____

_____

_____

_____

_____

_____

_____

_____

_____

_____

_____

_____

_____

_____

A POWERFUL INSTRUMENT

The Word of God, spoken and written, is the most powerful instrument known to man. God spoke, and the world came into existence; a creation which man's most sophisticated technology cannot measure. Not today. Not ever. Only God's mind could comprehend it. Because God is infinite, His word has not and will not lose its power. It continues to create as bold, believing men and women of God continue to proclaim it. As we will see later, the power of His word in us is revolutionary. However, His word has power inherently.

For example look more closely at John 1:1-4. Here, we are reminded of the fantastic power revealed through God's Word and God's Son.

To what extent have you experienced a revelation of God's power through His Word? Describe an incident in which God's Word empowered you to share your personal faith with someone.

RENEWING THE INNER MAN

In Romans 12:1-2, Paul said the following: "Therefore, I urge you, brothers, in view of God's mercy, to offer your bodies as living sacrifices, holy and pleasing to God--this is your spiritual act of worship. Do not conform any longer to the pattern of this world, but be transformed by the renewing of your mind. Then you will be able to test and approve what God's will is – His good, pleasing and perfect will." It is so easy to get caught up in the pressures and pleasures of this world that we find little time left to spend reflecting on eternal values. If we are to be transformed, we must cooperate with God by getting alone with God and giving Him our undivided attention, so that He can do the transforming.

It is so easy to get caught up in the pressures and pleasures of this world that we find little time left to spend reflecting on eternal values. If we are to be transformed we must cooperate with God by getting alone with God and giving Him our undivided attention, so that He can do the transforming.

In 2 Corinthians 4:16, Paul reminds us "Therefore we do not lose heart. Though outwardly we are wasting away, yet inwardly we are being renewed day by day." In order for this renewing to take place, we must discipline ourselves by meeting daily with God.

What specific activities are crowding out your time with God? In what ways is your daily reading of the Word renewing your mind and Spirit?

_____

_____

_____

_____

_____

_____

_____

_____

_____

_____

_____

_____

_____

_____

_____

_____

_____

_____

_____

_____

_____

_____

WORKING ON RENEWING
THE INNER MAN

In 1 Timothy 4:7-16 we find how important it is to discipline ourselves for the purpose of godliness. Paul writes, "For physical training is of some value, but godliness has value for all things, holding promise for both the present life and the life to come" (verse 8).

If we really want to be useful to the Master, we need to take special notice of 2 Timothy 2:21 where Paul advises us that "If a man cleanses himself. . .he will be an instrument for noble purposes, made holy, useful to the Master and prepared to do any good work." In the 119th Psalm, which is an outstanding chapter on the importance of the Word, David says, "I have hidden your word in my heart that I might not sin against you" (verse 9). And it is through the hiding of the word in *our* hearts that we became cleansed and transformed.

Unfortunately, the book "most sold" in the world — the Bible — is also the least read. I have heard several seasoned ministers say, "In years past those who became believers had a basic knowledge of the Judeo-Christian doctrine and the value system of the 10 commandments. This is no longer true… they come to us with a complete vacuum of Bible understanding."

How would you describe your overall understanding of the Bible? In what ways have you been cleansing yourself before beginning your meditation times with God?

_____

_____

_____

_____

_____

_____

_____

_____

_____

_____

_____

_____

_____

_____

_____

_____

_____

_____

_____

_____

_____

LED BY THE SPIRIT

As we meditate on the Word of God, we began to
see and to learn about the attributes of God and
specifically of Jesus, who is God's only Son. Jesus
often said, "If you have seen me, you have seen
the Father." This scripture helps us to see and
recognize His attributes of humility, obedience,
and servanthood. These qualities set an example
for us of being forgiving and unselfish just as He is
forgiving and unselfish.

In Galatians 5:16 we are advised to "live by the
Spirit" and if we do, we will not carry out the
desires of the flesh. As we are led by the Spirit and
guided by the Spirit by being in the Word, we
become involved with God. We learn to cooperate.
We allow His divine power to change our lives.

*Can you identify several times in the last few days
when you have allowed the desires of the flesh to take
over and prevent God's Spirit from leading you? How
does selfishness keep you from doing God's will in your
life?*

THERE IS NO MAGIC
TO MEDITATION

In our meditations, we should not look for a
method or a system, but cultivate an attitude, an
outlook of faith, openness, attention, reverence,
expectation, supplications, trust, joy. All these
permeate our being with love insofar as our living
faith tells us we are in the presence of God, that
we live in Christ, that in the Spirit of God we see
God our Father without seeing.

Faith is the bond that unites us to Him in the Spirit
who gives us light and love. Meditation is sometimes quite difficult. We should not judge the
value of our meditation by how we feel. A hard
and apparently fruitless meditation may in fact be
much more valuable than one that is easy, happy,
enlightened and seems to be a big success.

*Some believe that 90% of everything is attitude. Keep-
ing that thought in mind, how has your attitude affected your time alone with God? To what extent have
these thoughts concerning meditation affected your
desire to practice God's presence throughout the day?
Can you recall a season when time spent in God's Word
seemed hard or fruitless, but turned out to be very
meaningful and helpful?*

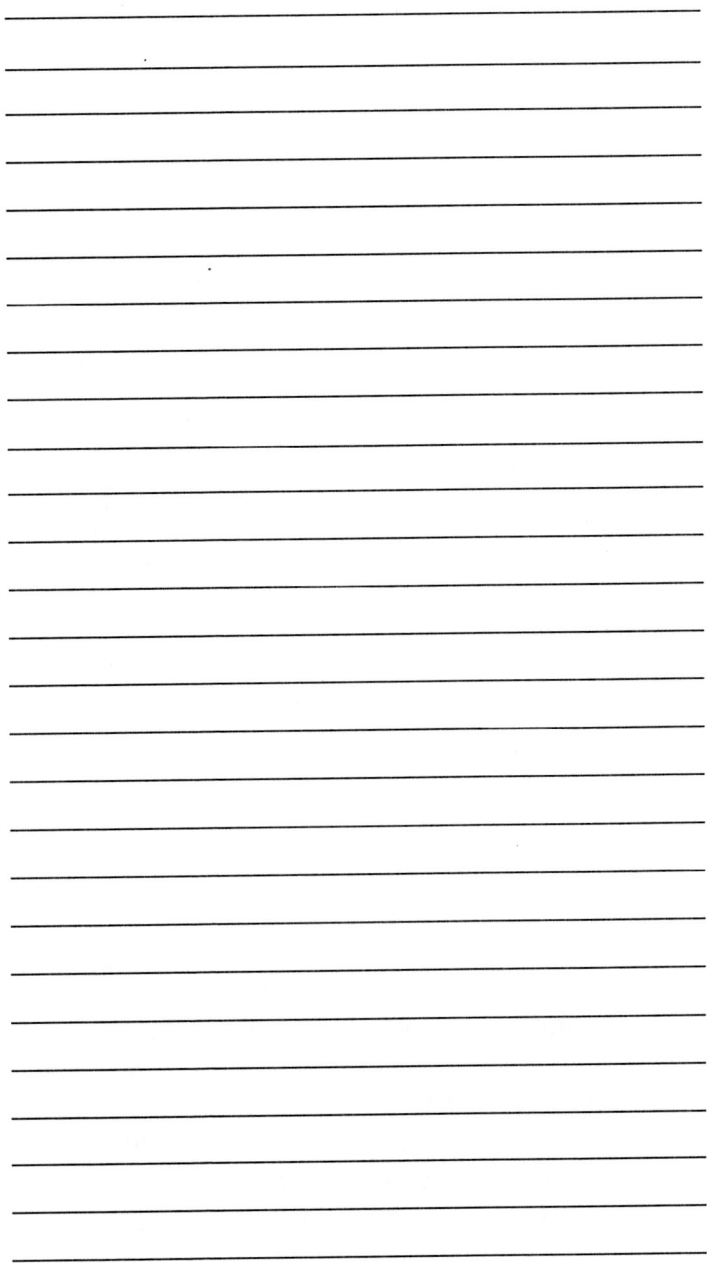

MEMORIZING THE WORD

Colossians 3:16 states, "Let the word of Christ dwell in you richly as you teach and admonish one another with all wisdom. . ." This certainly is one of the benefits of memorizing the Word. David, who was identified as a man after God's own heart, reminded us in Psalms 1:1-2, "Blessed is the man who does not walk in the counsel of the wicked or stand in the way of sinners or sit in the seat of mockers. But his delight is in the law of the LORD, and on his law he meditates day and night."

As we meditate, we find we can remember what we are trying to memorize more easily, especially if there is frequent reviewing taking place. It also will surprise you how God brings the same scriptures to mind in your conversations during the day as you share your deeper thoughts.

Can you recall two or three scriptures that you memorized when you were younger which have had special meaning to you over the years? What specific approach do you find most productive in memorizing scripture? What goals would you like to put into place that will help you increase your memorization of God's Word?

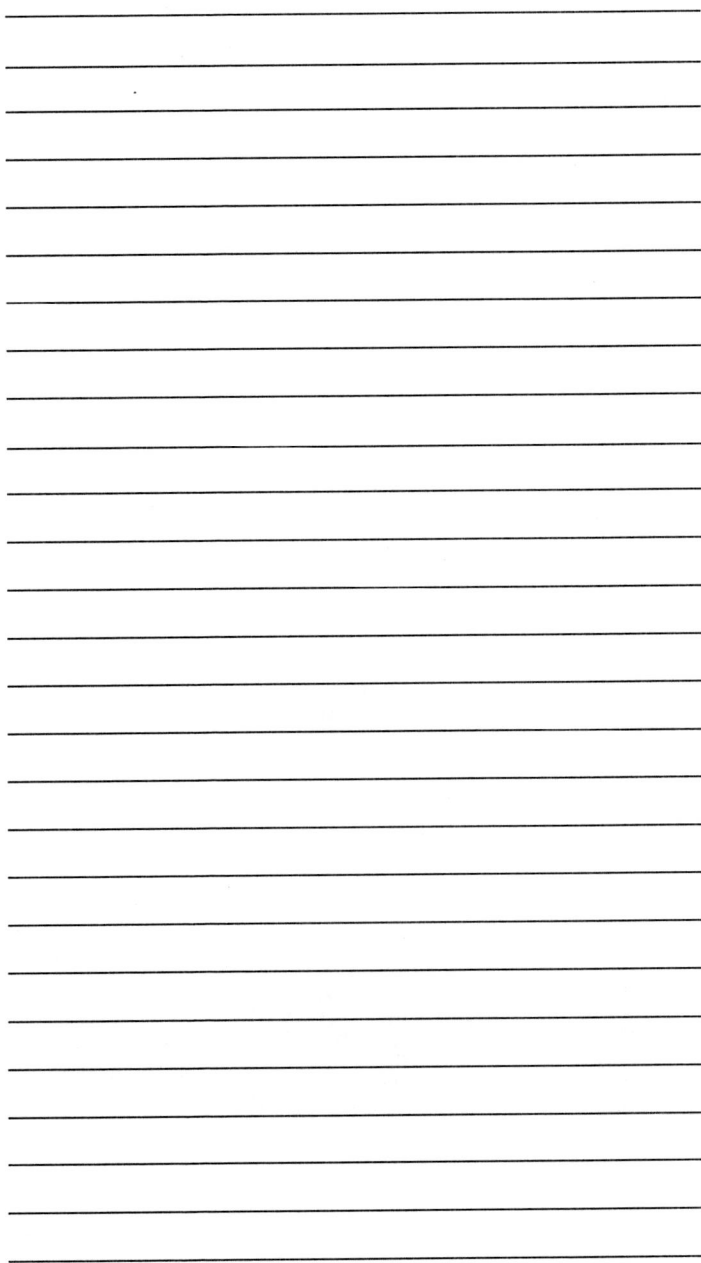

BEWARE OF LEGALISM

I was raised with a very wrong concept of who God really is. The truth is that all of us suffer from a wrong concept of God. It's very difficult to worship a God that is distorted and unknown. My son has often said, "You tell me what your concept of God is, and I'll tell you what your walk with God is like."

If our concept of God is narrow and out of balance, we will have a difficult time worshiping, loving and serving Him. We need to learn as much about God and His nature and character as we can in order to break free from some of our childish thoughts of who He is and what He does.

Do you know the things God likes and if so, could you list several of them? Have you suffered from a small and perhaps legalistic concept of God? If so, list some of those ideas and compare them with what the Bible tells us about God's character.

WHOLE-HEARTED DETERMINATION

"But seek first his kingdom and his righteousness, and all these things will be given to you as well" (Matt. 6:33). As we seek to have unbroken fellowship with God in Christ, throughout the day we will begin to understand how important it is to meet early in the morning to secure his presence. It is a discipline, but it is not a do-it-yourself program. We need to have our hearts receptive morning by morning so that the Holy Spirit can quicken the Word to our hearts and teach us the truths that will shape our lives.

This requires wholehearted determination, not a halfhearted interest. God's Word makes it very clear that He hates a lukewarm heart attitude. We are also encouraged to do things that bless and please God with all our might.

What do you discern as the difference between doing it all by yourself and an approach which not only requires discipline but a dependence on the Holy Spirit? How do you manage to seek first the kingdom of heaven in this fast-moving, crazy world?

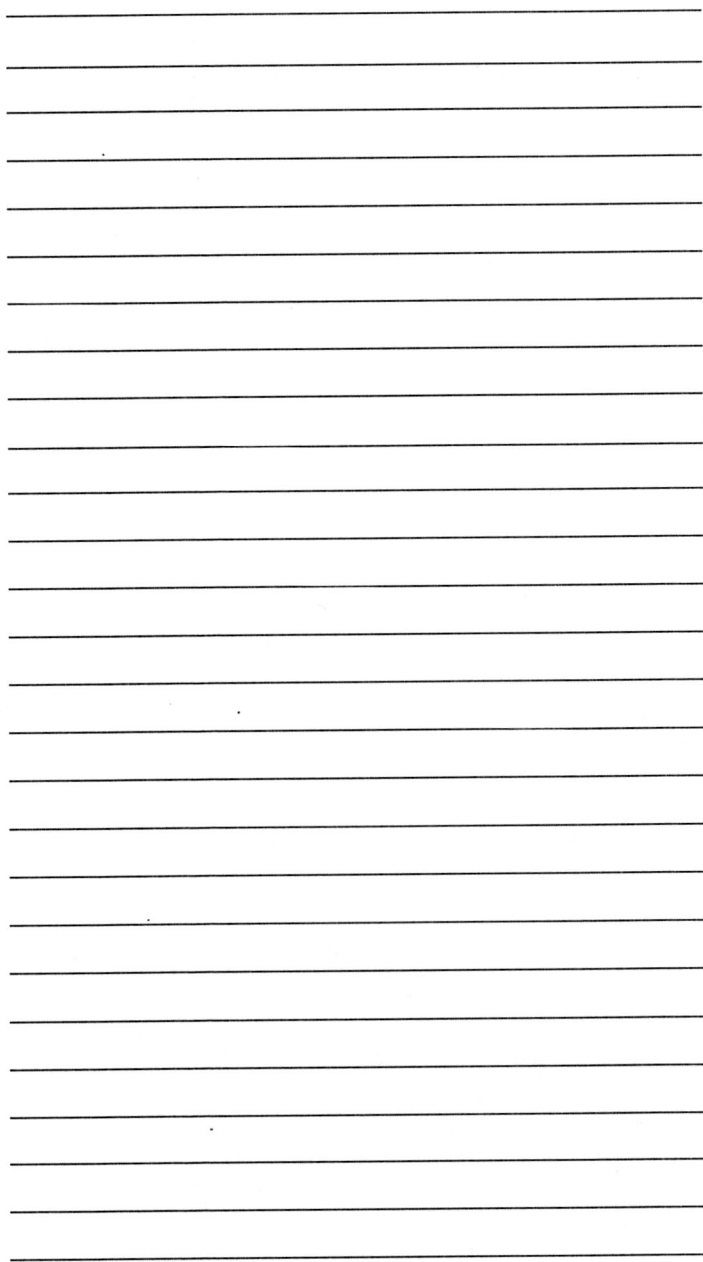

A DIVINE CHALLENGE

In 1 Corinthians 9:24-27, Paul reminds us of the importance of running the race of life well. In fact we are to run in such a way that we may win. We can liken Bible meditation to training for a race. In our training, we must run with intensity. We must push our physical body if we want to grow in the ability to run.

Next we must also run with frequency. You cannot run occasionally and expect to improve. Finally while we are running we must build up our endurance by running a little farther each time, thereby increasing our distance.

This very same concept can be applied to our spiritual growth. In Hebrew 12:1, Paul reminds us that we are to "throw off everything that hinders. . .and run with perseverance the race marked out for us."

In what ways are you including intensity, frequency, and endurance to strengthen your time alone with God? Are you able to identify some items that are hindering your ability to have intimate quiet times? Are you willing to remove them?

THE MORNING HOUR

In the morning, O LORD, you hear my voice; in the morning I lay my requests before you and wait in expectation (Psalms 5:3).

Morning has always been considered the best time for personal worship or quiet time. If we were playing in a concert, we would not tune our instrument after the concert was over. So it is with our hearts. We should use the morning time to practice close fellowship with God. To abide in Him and His presence, to be doing His will and pleasing Him, this must be accomplished as a regular practice if we are truly devoted to Him.

Each one of us is unique, therefore apply this concept to your life in such a way as to be beneficial to you. For example, if you work nights you may want to switch when you have your quiet time.

"The Sovereign LORD has given me an instructed tongue, to know the word that sustains the weary. He wakens me morning by morning, wakens my ear to listen like one being taught" (Isaiah 50:4). Other translations speak of having the tongue of the learned or wise. It is my firm belief that this can best be accomplished through effective Bible meditation.

Explain how you have been able to instruct a weary friend by using information from the Bible. How has being alone with God increased your wisdom?

_____

_____

_____

_____

_____

_____

_____

_____

_____

_____

_____

_____

_____

_____

_____

_____

_____

_____

_____

_____

_____

_____

REPENTANCE

In 2 Peter 3:9, we learn that "The Lord is not slow in keeping His promise, as some understand slowness. He is patient with you, not wanting anyone to perish, but everyone to come to repentance."

True repentance causes us to turn away from sin when we realize how much it breaks God's heart. This is one of the keys to entering the kingdom. Peter, after his first sermon, challenged the crowd to "Repent and be baptized, every one of you, in the name of Jesus Christ for the forgiveness of your sins. And you will receive the gift of the Holy Spirit" (Acts 2:38).

Repentance is a lifelong process not a onetime event. As we take time daily to repent and seek forgiveness, we keep our hearts pure and avoid bitterness from finding a home in our hearts. When we repent, according to God's guidelines, we turn from what we have done and avoid doing it again.

Can you list some of the main reasons that you hate to sin? Can you identify a besetting sin that continues to surface in your life? Are you willing to take it before the Lord in true repentance and stop it from coming back?

IT'S A WONDERFUL LIFE

Often we are so scheduled and weighed down by the cares of this life that we fail to fully appreciate life in all its wonder. We need to learn how to not miss the glory of the moment. As we begin to recognize the joy of being alive and refreshed, life becomes wonderful.

Joy comes when we put Jesus first, others second and ourselves last. We need to capture our heart's true experience and enjoy the thrill of living. It is so easy to allow life's problems to dull our senses and cause us to go through life numb and unappreciative. Little recorded steps of progress tends to encourage us and cause us to feel better.

Do you remember this line from an old hymn? "Count your many blessings, name them one by one, and it will surprise you what the Lord hath done." The best way to improve your state of mind is to think on good thoughts. There is another hymn that tells us to "Trust and obey, for there's no other way, to be happy in Jesus but to trust and obey."

What kind of worldly thoughts and activities have you participated in that have had a dulling effect on your senses? Review the activities of this last week and list two or three that have brought you the most joy.

_____

_____

_____

_____

_____

_____

_____

_____

_____

_____

_____

_____

_____

_____

_____

_____

_____

_____

_____

_____

_____

_____

_____

STUDY TO SHOW
YOURSELF APPROVED

As a very young man I memorized 2 Timothy 2:15: "Do your best to present yourself to God as one approved, a workman who does not need to be ashamed and who correctly handles the word of truth."

It has been one of my foundational scriptures and has been repeated many times as I have taught about the importance of God's Word. Great things are possible to the one who knows God's will and wills it with all of his heart. Our challenge is not only to read the Word but also to do it.

Aren't you blessed when you are around a person who walks what he talks? I for one would much rather see a sermon lived out in someone's life than to hear someone preach one. I am especially turned off when someone says one thing and then does something entirely different

Think about a particular person whose words and actions rarely match. What are your feelings toward that person? Can you think of a message where the person sharing did not correctly handle the word of truth? What happened in your life as a result of this?

How have you been able to come to a clearer understanding of the thought or idea?

_____

_____

_____

_____

_____

_____

_____

_____

_____

_____

_____

_____

_____

_____

_____

_____

_____

_____

_____

_____

_____

NO SUCH THING
AS INSTANT MATURITY

Over the years I have observed a grievous mistake taking place when people assume they are mature or totally changed simply by inviting Jesus into their heart. Growing into Christian maturity is a process usually requiring years of struggle on our part. Sometimes it is three steps forward and two steps backward.

For me there have been a few mountaintop experiences and a lot of valleys. I made a lot of growth when I found out that God liked me. You see, I knew He hated sin and I sinned, so I couldn't imagine that He liked me. It took a long time for me to believe that God not only liked me, He loved me unconditionally.

Paul the apostle is very careful to make sure that new converts are not placed in leadership roles in the church until they have matured and demonstrated a track record of appropriate conduct. I realize that we are all very different and we mature at varied rates. But the main point of this meditation is that it does not happen over night. After 50 years of adult life, I still find myself wondering if I will ever grow up.

Think about your own maturity for a moment. Can you identify areas that still need some work? Is there a special friend you really enjoy hanging out with? Do you believe God feels the same way toward you? Are you convinced that God likes you and likes to be with you? If not what can you do to change your understanding?

WORSHIP THE LORD

He alone is the only uncreated being in the entire universe that deserves to be worshiped. Worship the Lord with your whole heart. Rehearse some of His many wonderful attributes. Recount your many blessing and enjoy his presence. Praise him with enthusiasm. Employ all of your being in the act of worship. Remember you are a part of the orchestra not the audience when you worship God. Never feign devotion.

Allow your spirit to be released into unabashed praise of God as you enter into worship. Worship music takes on many forms. Some think the volume is most important; others think it should follow some specific form. Still others think it must be beautiful organ music. Worship may include any of these, but above all, it is the attitude of our heart.

Where do you find the most intimate type of worship taking place in your life? Can you identify a time in your life when worship moved to a new level? Have you allowed anything or anyone to take first place in your life which may actually be identified as an idol?

CONTROLLED BY THE SPIRIT

In Ephesians 5:18, Paul admonishes us, "Do not get drunk on wine, which leads to debauchery. Instead, be filled with the Spirit."

The real emphasis here is not so much the evil of drink but the necessity to be mastered, gripped, and controlled by the Holy Spirit. This scripture has much power and meaning in my life. It requires total surrender to the leading and guidance of the Holy Spirit in every aspect of my life.

In today's world there are many different opinions as to what it means to be filled with or baptized by the Holy Spirit. I do not think it appropriate to take a particular side or position on this subject, but I do believe we can agree that in order to grow and become more Christ-like, we must be empowered by the Holy Spirit and surrender our thoughts to His control. Would you care to join me by inviting the Holy Spirit to take complete control of your life?

Several years ago when I was attempting to grow in my understanding of the importance of the Holy Spirit's place in the Godhead, I underlined every place in the New Testament where the Holy

Spirit was mentioned. I was truly amazed at how much the influence of the Holy Spirit is spread throughout the pages.

How much of your life is controlled by the Holy Spirit? Can you describe what you believe to be the best evidence of a person being filled with the Spirit?

_____

_____

_____

_____

_____

_____

_____

_____

_____

_____

_____

_____

_____

_____

_____

_____

_____

_____

_____

_____

STEPS TOWARD HOLINESS

Examine yourself by asking the question: is there anything that hinders my obedience to God? If the answer is affirmative, do whatever it takes to change that.

Remove every idol in your life. If you have something you couldn't bear to lose, give it away. Refuse to let any worldly interest rule your heart. Never go to bed angry and clean your heart from every root of bitterness.

Say no to sin. Always stop it before it has a chance to become a fixture in your life. Always maintain a clear conscience. Guard your heart from the vices and evil of this world. The lust of the eyes and the pride of life is everywhere.

How would you describe your personal lust of the eyes? Are there still pride issues that you struggle with on a daily basis? When you go to bed angry, how do you feel the next day toward the person you were angry with?

GOD'S WORD IS A SEED

Matthew 13 contains several parables about God's Word being a seed. There is much to ponder in these illustrations, from the apparent insignificance of a small seed to the large tree it springs into. A number of truths also come from these parables, including faith, patience and fruitfulness. God's Word is laced with power. When we learn that God can do what He says in His Word, then we have found one of the secrets of Bible meditation.

We still have a vital role in this seed planting business. The condition of the soil is most important if the seed is to germinate and produce fruit. If the soil is not good, the multiplication does not take place. The same thing is true with regards to our heart. If we are not open and ready to receive truth, very little change will take place.

What is the condition of your heart? Is it open and ready to receive new revelation? What does it mean to you to have a teachable spirit? In what ways would you want to improve your teachable spirit?

THE JOY OF JOURNALING

The light went on for me when I realized that several of the books of the Bible are merely examples of godly journaling. David's Psalms are examples of his daily ups and downs. Solomon's journaling gave us Ecclesiastics and Job has his daily dialogue with God. Few men and women have accomplished godly growth without journaling in some form. If we care enough about our lives to want to grow, then we need to record where we are and where we are going.

There are many beautiful journals on the market today. If you shop carefully you can find one to suit your personal style of journaling. Many take a different shape than the one proposed in this book, but that's just fine. The main encouragement is to get started and develop a form of journaling that fits your personality.

Do you have a good understanding of where you are spiritually? If not, what plans do you have to get to where you want to be? Why not review some of your writings to see if there are any threads or insights that keep reappearing?

LEARNING TO BE OBEDIENT

"This will happen if you diligently obey the LORD your God" (Zechariah 6:15).

God often speaks to us in ways that are easy to misunderstand. Loren Cunningham, founder of Youth With a Mission, wrote a book entitled, "Is That Really You God?" Some of the godliest men I know still have trouble clearly discerning if it really is God speaking to them. It gets much easier when God writes it out and makes it clear in His Word.

We need to get into the habit of saying, "speak Lord," and then, take time to listen. When we get a clear word through meditation, we must learn to obey joyfully, instantly and completely. Let me interject a caution at this point. I have seen some people throw all reason and prudent behavior aside when they believe God has spoken. This has done much harm to the person and to the body of Christ. I have learned to compare all of my personal guidance with the principles set forth in the Bible, before I act on something that may be questionable.

Can you recall an incident in which you (or someone else) had guidance you thought was from God, but later it turned out to be false or inappropriate? How about searching God's Word to find other books of the Bible that are good examples of journaling.

LIFE IS NOT FAIR

"I consider that our present sufferings are not worth comparing with the glory that will be revealed in us" (Romans 8:18). Some people seem to be born on third base and go through life thinking that they hit a triple, while others get up to bat with two strikes against them.

This life is not fair. The sooner we figure that out the happier we will be. Paul reminds us in 2 Corinthians 12:9, "But He said to me, 'My grace is sufficient for you, for my power is made perfect in weakness.' Therefore I will boast all the more gladly about my weaknesses, so that Christ's power may rest on me."

It's not life's circumstance that really count but how we handle them. We must keep uppermost in mind that "God is our refuge and strength, an ever-present help in trouble" (Psalm 46:1).

Think about some recent suffering or difficult circumstance. How has your character been improved by this? Can you think of any weakness in your life that you, like Paul, can boast about? What advantage over others have you had because of your parents?

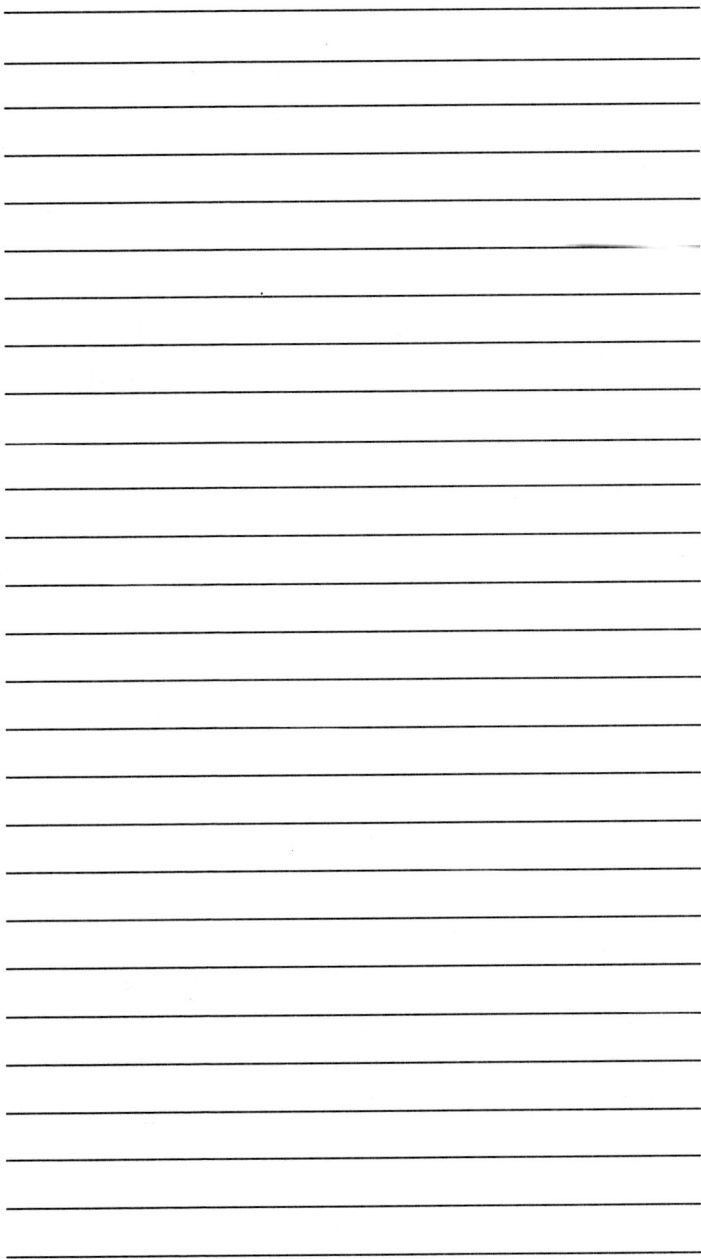

PRACTICE HIS PRESENCE

". . .the Spirit of truth. The world cannot accept Him, because it neither sees Him nor knows Him. But you know Him, for He lives with you and will be in you" (John 14:17).

One of the most compelling and challenging experiences of my life is to attempt to practice His presence all day, every day. To desire a heart in which the Spirit of God abounds is a goal worth seeking. Seeing Him in the midst of all that you do and say requires constant discipline. I certainly have not arrived but I am pressing in to make practicing His presence a life goal.

"On that day you will realize that I am in my Father, and you are in me, and I am in you" (John 14:20).

Practice His presence for a single day and see if it makes a difference in the way you respond. Try not to be discouraged if it appears to be harder than you thought. Like anything else, it improves with practice.

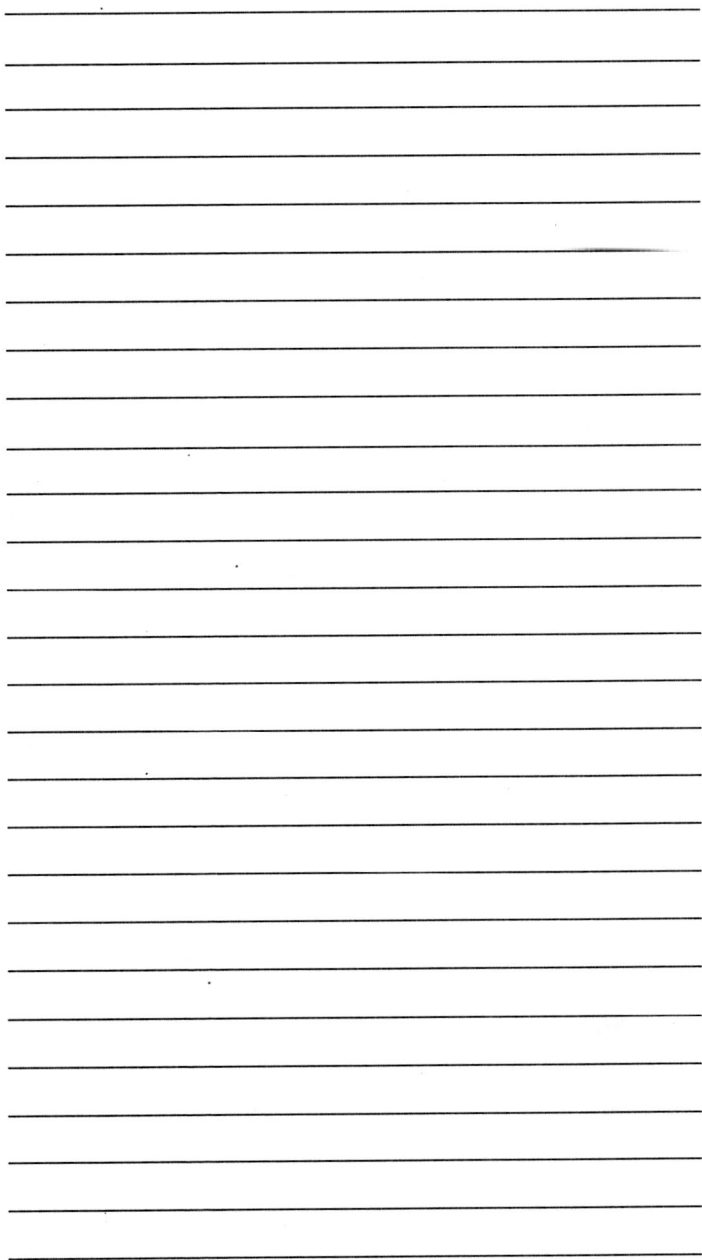

ALONE WITH GOD

"Very early in the morning, while it was still dark, Jesus got up, left the house and went off to a solitary place, where He prayed" (Mark 1:35).

John uses the significant expression "went off to a solitary place." Jesus often went entirely by Himself. Relationships with people can draw us away from God and exhaust our energies. It is essential for Christians to set themselves apart to think, reflect and prioritize their lives.

In this secret "solitary place," we begin to realize what a blessing it is to have God all alone and to know that God has us all alone to Himself. Often we don't recognize our pride, envy, and laziness until we get alone before God.

Is your time alone with God growing and improving? If your time is not getting better, can you discover the hindrances that are standing in the way?

LIVING LIFE AT THE NEXT LEVEL

One of my life purposes is to excel and be the best I can be. I assume that all of us want to be the best we can be. I enjoy reflecting on the thought that it's time to be great before it's too late. If we are to move to the next level, we must first determine where we are and what the next level will be.

As we record in our journals what God reveals to us through His word, His principles, and His purpose, we can begin to see the plans that He has for our lives and the means He has provided to get there.

What plans have you uncovered that God has for your life? When you think about wanting to be the best, which field or gift would you like most to improve?

TO KNOW HIM AND
TO MAKE HIM KNOWN

All too often we attempt to tell people about God when we really don't know Him ourselves. It's very hard to make Him known unless you personally know Him. Meditating on His word will help you to know His likes and His dislikes, how He feels about sin and so on.

Realizing God is omniscient keeps us from trying to hide from Him and helps us believe that He loves us and rewards those who diligently serve Him. As you delight in His Word, changes will take place without a great deal of effort. God's judgments will not come as a surprise as you learn His standards through the scriptures.

It is very difficult to make an introduction of the speaker at a banquet if you know very little about him. So it is with God. If you attempt to introduce Him to someone, it really helps to know Him well.

Getting to know God is one of my primary purposes for existing. Would you like to make it one of yours too? Can you list three ways you have come to know God better?

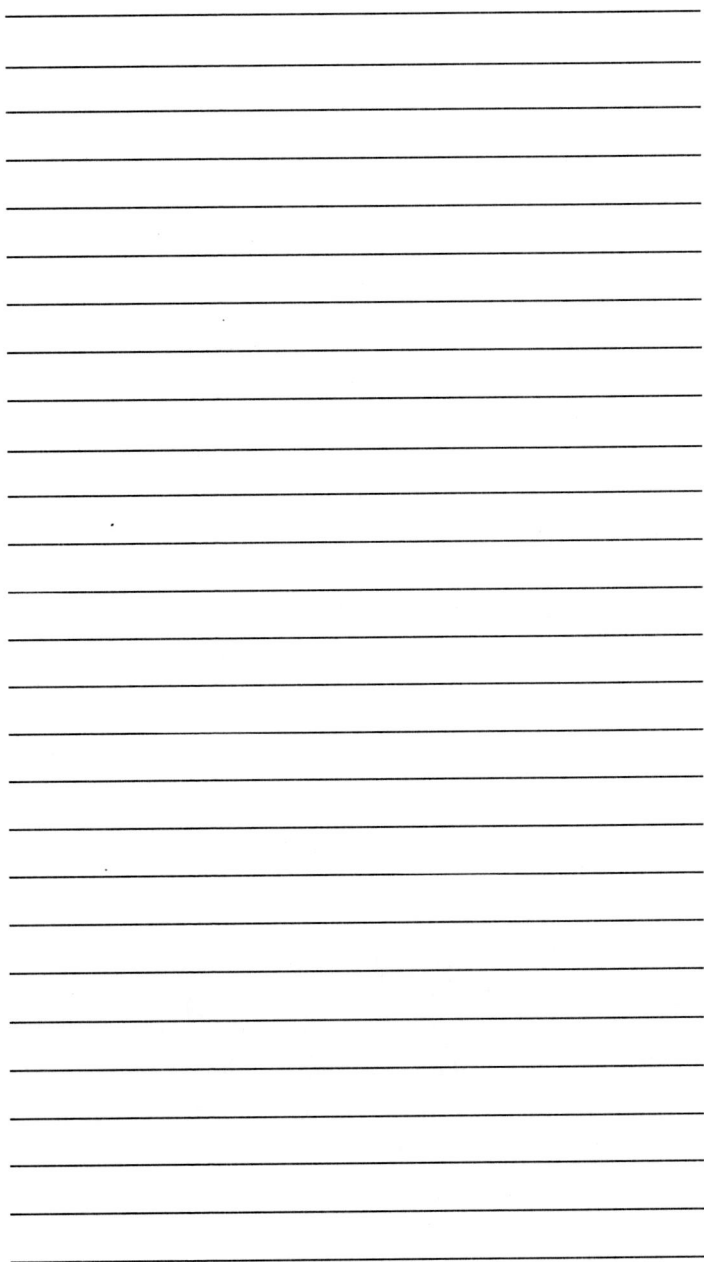

YOUR WORD HAVE I
HID IN MY HEART

"Oh how I love your law! I meditate on it all day long" (Psalms 119:97). "I have taken an oath and confirmed it, that I will follow your righteous laws" (Psalms 119:106). "I obey your statutes, for I love them greatly (Psalms 119:167).

Psalms 119 is *the* place God's word teaches us the importance of the Word. David makes it very clear how important it is to honor and keep God's Word hidden in our hearts (verse 11). In this chapter, the Word of God becomes rich and inexhaustible material for having communion with the Living God. It will lift you into God's presence.

Seek the Holy Spirit to assist you in elevating your devotional life to the level revealed in the Psalms. Let all that God's Word brings to us, make us more earnest in longing to carry that Word to others.

Can you think of one or more scriptures that you have hidden in your heart in the past few days? David is known as a man after God's heart. What does this mean to you? What do you see as the major difference between just reading the Word and hiding it in your heart?

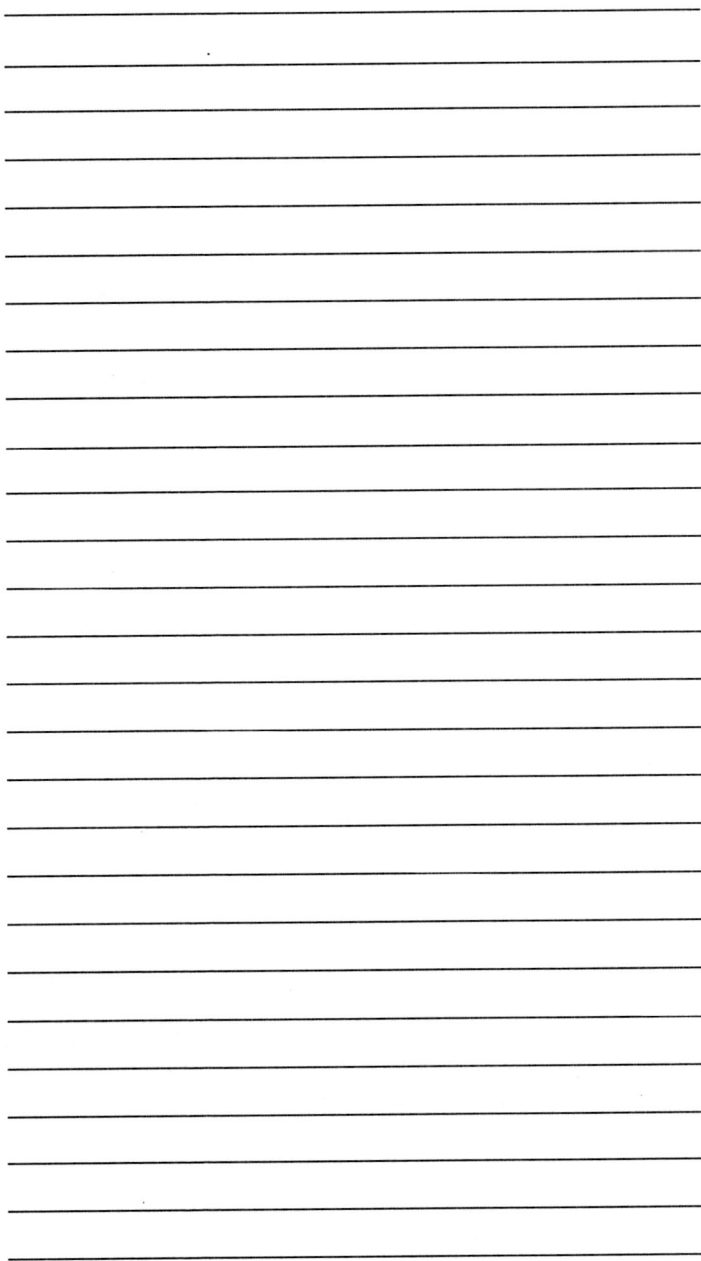

THE ART OF MEDITATION

"I meditate on your precepts" (Psalms 119:15). Meditation is turning our hearts toward God and seeking to make His Word a part of our life. Whatever the heart truly believes, it allows to master and rule our life.

The Word is meant to bring us into His presence. Here in solitude we muse or dwell at length on the meaning of these scriptures for our personal lives. Personal application takes a prominent place. In meditation the chief purpose is to appropriate and experience what we read.

Meditation should lead to prayer. "May the words of my mouth and the meditation of my heart be pleasing in your sight, O LORD, my Rock and my Redeemer" (Psalms 19:14).

How can you ensure that the words of your mouth and the meditations of your heart are more acceptable in God's sight? Can you show family members how God's Word being hidden in your heart has improved your actions?

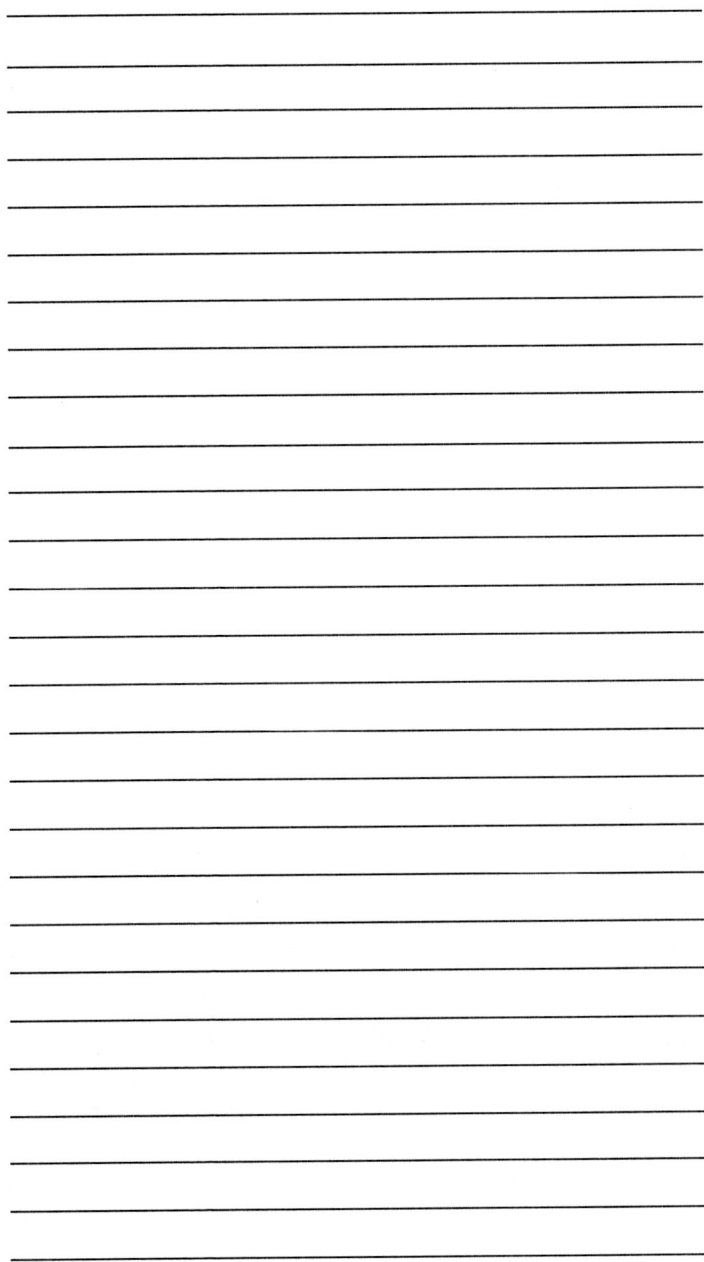

THE UNEXAMINED
LIFE IS NOT WORTH LIVING

Beware of sacrificing your life for worthless things. You will find that it all amounts to nothing. Remember there are no U-Haul trailers following anybody's hearse. In 1 Corinthians 3:11, Paul tells us, "For no one can lay any foundation other than the one already laid, which is Jesus Christ."

Don't do anything that is not built on Him. Take a hard look. Examine your life to see how much energy you are spending on worthless stuff that has little or no eternal value. Spending time alone with God in His Word will help you to look at life through God's eyes. Do you have a personal mission statement? Are you taking time every morning to keep your activities properly prioritized? In life, it's often not what you know, but who you know. So get to know God and His ways.

Do you have a personal mission statement? Are you spending time every morning to keep your activities properly prioritized? In life, it's often not what you know, but who you know. How is spending more time in the Word helping you get to know God better?

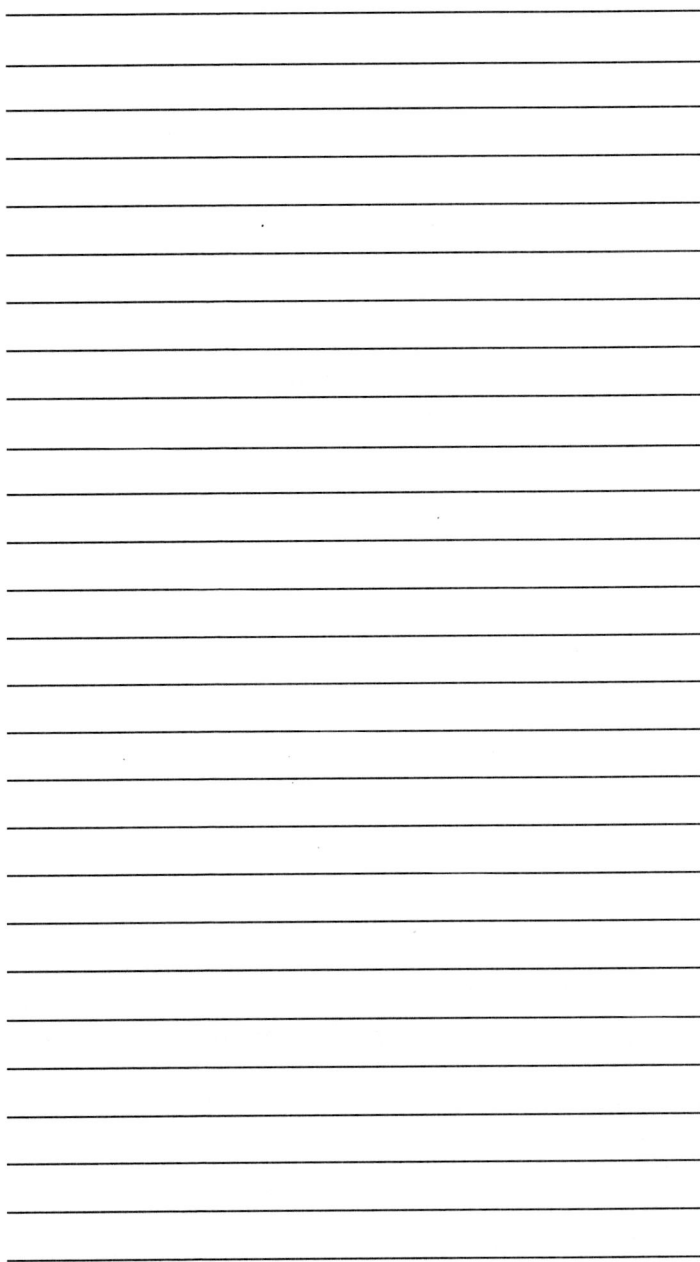

CIRCUMSTANCES ARE
NOT IMPORTANT

"Though the fig tree does not bud and there are no grapes on the vines, though the olive crop fails and the fields produce no food, though there are no sheep in the pen and no cattle in the stalls, yet I will rejoice in the LORD, I will be joyful in God my Savior. The Sovereign LORD is my strength; He makes my feet like the feet of a deer, He enables me to go on the heights" (Habakkuk 3:17-19).

We often place far too much emphasis on our circumstances. We are reminded that really nothing can separate us from the love of God. As my wife Betty was in the later stages of cancer this became one of her favorite passages. Our lasting joy comes from the Lord, not from circumstances but from our inner strength of character. The older I get the less important each set of circumstances seems to me. It is much easier to trust in the Lord when you look at things from an eternal perspective.

Are there circumstances that are presently weighing you down? Look at them and ask yourself, "How much difference will this make 100 years from now?" How have you been able to go to new heights with the Lord by following in His footsteps?

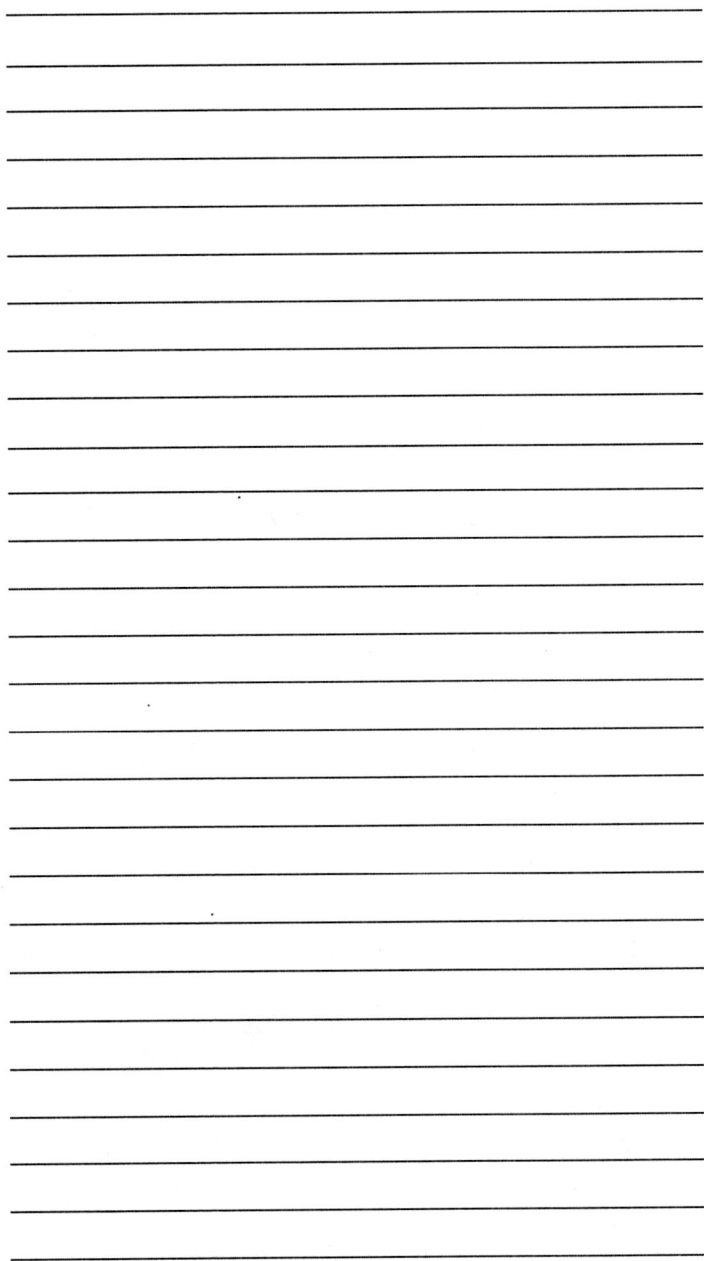

LEARNING TO COVENANT

"All the ways of the LORD are loving and faithful for those who keep the demands of his covenant" (Psalms 25:10). The secret of the Lord is for those who fear Him. He will make them know His covenant.

It is important to realize that everything God does is based on covenant. All too often we enter into relationships, such as marriage, with a contract frame of mind instead of a covenant that is eternal in nature and should never be broken.

In our society today many people look for a back door, an easy way out, in case they don't like what is happening. The concept, " My word is my bond," has been so badly eroded that it has modest meaning today. When we make a promise or a covenant, we need to understand the seriousness of what we have done and make sure we carry through with it in a responsible way.

God made a covenant with Abraham, a covenant He kept. He made a covenant with us as well, to never leave or forsake us. We need to take more seriously our covenant with Him. In His Word He reveals that the covenant bond is the highest personal relationship possible.

Can you think of one or more covenants or promises that you have failed to follow through on? What type of back door have you been holding onto in case things don't work out?

_____

_____

_____

_____

_____

_____

_____

_____

_____

_____

_____

_____

_____

_____

_____

_____

_____

_____

_____

MAKING MEMORIES

Our natural minds are designed in such a way as to cause us to have more and more difficulties in remembering specific details. I have a set of keys with a tab on the ring which says, "Keys I have not lost yet." It seems that more and more of my energy goes into finding misplaced items. It's all a part of the aging process. As a result of this I have to work at being more organized and designating specific places to keep certain items.

There is another side to this memory business. The more we fill our minds and hearts with godly memories the more likely we will be able to pull up memories to help us resolve life situations. The Bible instructs us to spend time thinking on or dwelling on "whatever is true, whatever is noble, whatever is right, whatever is pure, whatever is lovely, whatever is admirable--if anything is excellent or praiseworthy--think about such things" (Philippians 4:8).

What are you filling your mind with? How much time do you spend in God's word, compared with the amount of time spent watching television?

PRAYING THE WORD

"Let me understand the teaching of your precepts; then I will meditate on your wonders" (Psalms 119:27). The procedure of praying back the Word of God was shared with me several years ago. Personalizing God's Word by praying it back to Him has greatly enhanced my life and my understanding of His Word.

As we pray it back to Him, He has a way of internalizing the Word to us and hiding it in our hearts. It causes the Word to be much more personal and meaningful when we pray.

"Remove from me scorn and contempt, for I keep your statutes" (Psalms 119:22).

Can you locate one of your favorite scriptures, personalize it, and pray it back to God? See if it is possible to pray for others with the same intensity that you pray for your own needs.

LEAVE ROOM FOR GOD

It is so important that we remain flexible and leave room for God to surprise us by breaking through with His power. We must realize that God is never caught off guard or surprised by some turn of events in our lives. He desires to have "elbow room" in our lives. We tend to make all kinds of plans, often leaving God out of the process. It's an excellent idea to seek God's counsel and pray for wisdom before entering into any major decision.

Make room for God to have His way in your life. Remember no matter how well you may think you know God, He may break through in a surprising way when you least expect it. It is so easy to rule God out of the equation, thinking He must be far too busy ruling the universe to be concerned about my insignificant problems.

What type of room are you leaving for God in your heart and mind to assist you in your daily walk? Are you able to recall a time when you were surprised by God?

LIVING SIMPLY

Paul reminds us, "I am not saying this because I am in need, for I have learned to be content whatever the circumstances" (Philippians 4:11). In America, our world is one of materialism and great pressure. We are often trying to "keep up with the Joneses." We need to ask ourselves the question: What difference would this make in eternity?

In my senior years, I am trying very hard to focus on those activities that have eternal significance. That's why I have chosen to expend the energy to write this material. My hope is that it will help you to focus on the vital things of this world and prepare you to rule and reign with Christ forever.

It is no small thing to simplify your life. Basic life patterns are hard to put aside. If you have been doing something a certain way for a number of years it takes a good deal of discipline and commitment to change things. This is where transformation through Bible meditation can be of great assistance. It will give you a fresh look at life and help you to see things in a new and different way.

To what extent are you interested in simplifying your life? Are you able to make a list of items that would simplify your life, and prioritize it in order to get you started?

_____

_____

_____

_____

_____

_____

_____

_____

_____

_____

_____

_____

_____

_____

_____

_____

_____

_____

_____

_____

_____

_____

_____

_____

FAITH'S PLACE IN THE WORD

"Consequently, faith comes from hearing the message, and the message is heard through the word of Christ" (Romans 10:17). The King James version may be more familiar, "So then faith cometh by hearing, and hearing by the Word of God."

Faith in God is crucial to the Christian life. Paul also reminds us that if we have the faith as a mustard seed, we can move mountains (Matthew 17:20). Do you have a mountain in your life that needs to be moved? God wants you to know you have a measure of faith resident within you. It needs to be acknowledged and acted upon. Remember nothing is impossible with God (Luke 1:37), but we have to place our mustard seed-sized faith into action.

Only God can change the nature of that seed so that it becomes a plant filled with power to push through the earth and grow into a strong tree that birds can sit upon. Be encouraged for we walk by faith not by sight.

"Now faith is being sure of what we hope for and certain of what we do not see" (Hebrews 11:1).

How has your faith been strengthened by meditating on the material contained in the pages of this book? Reread chapter 11 of Hebrews, then ask yourself this question. "How has my understanding of faith been broadened?"

_____

_____

_____

_____

_____

_____

_____

_____

_____

_____

_____

_____

_____

_____

_____

_____

_____

_____

_____

_____

_____

_____

MOMENTS OF DRYNESS

Let's be honest. We all have moments when we are confused, depressed and have a hard time figuring out which way is up. At times like this, we need to reread Isaiah 46:9: "Remember the former things, those of long ago; I am God, and there is no other; I am God, and there is none like me."

I have yet to meet a mature Christian who has not had days or weeks of dryness. One very helpful way to get through these difficult times is to acknowledge the fact they exist and will not remain forever.

Realize that it came to pass, it did not come to stay. Our problems are temporary and minor compared to the wonderful rich life waiting for us on the other side. It's time to focus on our blessings and not on our difficulties.

Over the years, what have you done in moments of dryness? Some seem to run around in circles, screaming and shouting! Take a few minutes now to outline your approach so you are prepared in advance whenever you face a dry time.

WHAT IS GOD LIKE?

"The God who made the world and everything in it is the Lord of heaven and earth and does not live in temples built by hands. And he is not served by human hands, as if he needed anything, because he himself gives all men life and breath and everything else" (Acts 17:24-25).

He is all-wise and all-knowing. He can do anything and everything we cannot do. He is immortal and infallible. God is a Spirit eternal and ever living. He has no beginning and no end. He is the essence of love. He is our righteous judge, totally just and fair. He is the creator of all and revealed Himself through Christ as our Father. He exists in nature but He isn't nature. As Jehovah we see Him as the One who caused everything else to be.

It is really naive to think we can know what God is like by reading a short paragraph, which describes a few of His character qualities. I have spent years meditating on His word and still feel very inadequate in my understanding of who He is. My only comfort comes from the understanding that I know more than I used to and want to spend the rest of my life getting to know Him better.

Can you identify concepts of God that have changed in your heart and mind over the last few weeks? To what extent do you feel comfortable seeing yourself as the temple of the living God?

_____

_____

_____

_____

_____

_____

_____

_____

_____

_____

_____

_____

_____

_____

_____

_____

_____

_____

_____

_____

_____

_____

RESTORATION OF INTIMACY WITH GOD

The Lord illustrates the restoration of intimacy with His people through the analogy of the Bride and Bridegroom. The passage in Revelation 19:7-9 tells of the wedding feast of the lamb. Jesus claims His Bride (the church) after she has made herself ready. When Jesus returns, His intimacy will be restored and we will be made one with God and Christ. Christ is our life and through Him we have life and have it more abundantly.

When God restores us He replaces our spiritual death with spiritual life. Not only do we receive a new type of life, but also we are encouraged to grow in it. It is a process requiring us to cooperate with God. As restoration takes place in our lives God's power is released to assist us to be all that we were designed to be.

Can you describe the level of intimacy that you have with God? What activity seems to encourage or enhance your intimacy with God?

TRUST IN THE LORD,
NOT IN YOURSELF

Trust is the belief in and reliance on the intricate strength, ability and surety of a person or thing. To trust in the Lord is to believe absolutely that what He says is true. Trust in the Lord and not in your wealth for financial security. Trust in the Lord and not in your physical strength. Trust in the Lord and not in political power or connections. Trust in the Lord and not in things you own or have built.

As we walk down life's pathway, it is normal to trust in those things that seem to work. The older and wiser you become, however, the more you discover the things that don't work. Sometimes it seems that's what life is all about – trying to discern things that work and things that don't. The objective of this book is to assist you in finding what works in life from the Word of God.

Can you make a list of the things you used to think worked, but no longer are willing to put your trust in? Several years ago I committed Proverbs 3:5 to memory. Will you look it up and try committing it to memory? I think you will find it most rewarding.

PUT GOD FIRST

"But Jesus would not entrust himself to them, for he knew. . .what was in a man" (John 2:24-25).

We must place our trust in God first. Jesus was careful not to put His trust in any person. Yet He was careful not to be bitter or suspicious of others. He was full of hope and often saw people in terms of their highest potential. If I put my trust in human beings first, the end result will be despair and hopelessness. We often insist that people be what they are incapable of being. Even putting complete trust in ourselves can lead to serious problems.

In Proverbs 3:5-6, we read, "Trust in the LORD with all your heart and lean not on your own understanding; in all your ways acknowledge Him, and He will make your paths straight."

Too often we see needs and immediately assume they are ours to meet. Our primary purpose is to study and seek to find out what God's needs are for us and then meet them.

Can you recall a time when you observed a need and assumed that it was your responsibility to solve the problem only to find out later, it was not all that help-

ful? Have unrealistic expectations ever caused you needless pain? If so, how might you do things differently next time?

_____

_____

_____

_____

_____

_____

_____

_____

_____

_____

_____

_____

_____

_____

_____

_____

_____

_____

_____

_____

_____

LEISURE TIME AND
YOUR QUIET TIME

How we spend our leisure time is important. It reveals our character. Each one of us has to develop our own character. It is during our leisure time when we are free to do as we please, free from rules and schedules, that our true character is revealed. Often we see the morning watch as interfering with our holiday pleasure. We find that the cares of this world often get in the way of our quiet time and it is most difficult to get back to being alone with God once the activities of the day gets underway.

As much as we need physical food every day while we are on holiday, we also need spiritual food. The world needs us to be its light twenty-four hours a day, seven days a week, which includes holidays. We need to be in communication with the fountain of all light every day anew.

As you search your heart, do you find a problem surfacing when you evaluate how you spend your leisure time? I have heard it said that Satan never takes a vacation. With that thought in mind, are there more effective things you can do with your leisure time and still enjoy life?

DO NOT WORRY

"So do not worry, saying, `What shall we eat?' or `What shall we drink?' or `What shall we wear?' For the pagans run after all these things, and your heavenly Father knows that you need them. But seek first His kingdom and His righteousness, and all these things will be given to you as well. Therefore do not worry about tomorrow, for tomorrow will worry about itself. Each day has enough trouble of its own" (Matthew 6:31-34).

Worry suggests a distraction, a preoccupation with things, causing anxiety, stress, and pressure. Which one of us by worrying can add a single moment to our lives? Our heavenly Father already knows all our needs, and He will give us all we need from day to day, if we live for Him and make the kingdom of God our primary concern.

Even though most of us are aware that worrying has no value, most of do a lot more worrying than we should. Can you list three things you have needlessly worried about in the past few days? Weeks? Months? What physical problems have you noticed in your life that have resulted from excessive worry?

PURE AND UNDEFILED RELIGION

"Religion that God our Father accepts as pure and faultless is this: to look after orphans and widows in their distress and to keep oneself from being polluted by the world" (James 1:27).

We are often confused about what New Testament Christianity is all about. We have come to the conclusion that church attendance is the name of the game. God has a different idea. He encourages us to be vessels of love and care for those who are in need, specifically orphans, widows, and those in prison. God has made it very clear that before the great white throne we will need to give a report with regards to our actions in this area.

What would your report look like if you were required to give one today? What are some things you would like to participate in that would improve your account? How has this section motivated you to change some of your behavior?

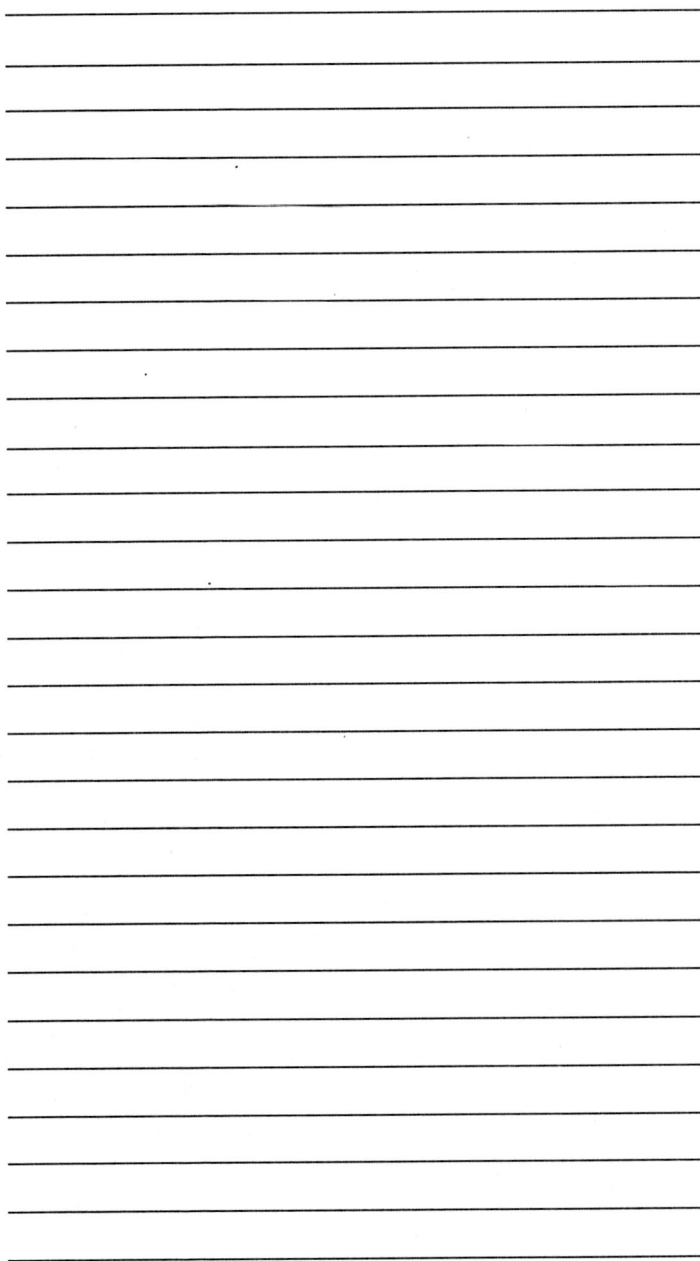

SIMPLE CHRISTIANITY

"Then the King will say to those on his right, `Come, you who are blessed by my Father; take your inheritance, the kingdom prepared for you since the creation of the world. For I was hungry and you gave me something to eat, I was thirsty and you gave me something to drink, I was a stranger and you invited me in, I needed clothes and you clothed me, I was sick and you looked after me, I was in prison and you came to visit me.'

"Then the righteous will answer him, `Lord, when did we see you hungry and feed you, or thirsty and give you something to drink? When did we see you a stranger and invite you in, or needing clothes and clothe you? When did we see you sick or in prison and go to visit you?' The King will reply, `I tell you the truth, whatever you did for one of the least of these brothers of mine, you did for me'" (Matthew 25:34-40).

As we find opportunity to serve and love those listed above in tangible ways, as we reach out to people we need to have as our focus that we are doing it to Christ and for Christ. Good works do not produce good character; good character produces good works. Over the years it has become more and more clear that this indeed is the mark of kingdom activity or simple Christianity.

Who among your many friends best exemplifies this kind of lifestyle? In the passage above, can you clearly identify the 'brother' in your life?

_____

_____

_____

_____

_____

_____

_____

_____

_____

_____

_____

_____

_____

_____

_____

_____

_____

_____

_____

_____

OVERCOMING TEMPTATION

"For this reason he had to be made like his brothers in every way, in order that he might become a merciful and faithful high priest in service to God, and that he might make atonement for the sins of the people. Because he himself suffered when he was tempted, he is able to help those who are being tempted" (Hebrews 2:17-18).

This is one of the reasons it is so important to set aside time to meet with God in the Word and prayer everyday. It's for your benefit, your well-being. When you are moving in the wisdom of the Word, in the power of the Spirit, directed by communication with Him in prayer, then you are a vessel fit for the Master's use.

Do you believe you have the same power to overcome temptation that Jesus had? To what extent do you think we can live a life free of sin if we have been born again?

YOU CANNOT SERVE
GOD AND RICHES

"No one can serve two masters. Either he will hate the one and love the other, or he will be devoted to the one and despise the other. You cannot serve both God and Money" (Matt. 6:24).

The enemy is weak in the presence of our strength. He will lose ground when we make a show of determination. We must choose whom we will serve. When we lose courage and give into the lusts of this world, the anger, rage and vindictiveness of the ruler of this dark world become great beyond all bounds. I have heard it said that God is the fastest checker player in the entire world because it is always your move. He has already done His part.

This concept of not serving two masters has troubled me much over the years. I guess it is because I see so much influence by those given over to money both inside and outside the body of Christ. I have wrestled with trying to live a balanced lifestyle for most of my life.

Does this bother you too? The key seems to be making Jesus Lord of all, including our finances. Are there pockets in your life where you are failing to surrender a portion of your control over finances to God?

_____

_____

_____

_____

_____

_____

_____

_____

_____

_____

_____

_____

_____

_____

_____

_____

_____

_____

_____

_____

_____

DYING TO SELF

"Put to death, therefore, whatever belongs to your earthly nature: sexual immorality, impurity, lust, evil desires and greed, which is idolatry. Because of these, the wrath of God is coming. You used to walk in these ways, in the life you once lived. But now you must rid yourselves of all such things as these: anger, rage, malice, slander, and filthy language from your lips. Do not lie to each other, since you have taken off your old self with its practices (Colossians 3:5-9).

And in Romans 8:8, we read, "Those controlled by the sinful nature cannot please God." For years I tried to improve my old nature instead of realizing I was to put it to death. This cost me a great deal of wasted time and energy. Finally as I meditated on God's Word, the difference became clear to me. The secret is to die daily to the old nature. The quicker this happens the better it is. We are to "put on the new self, which is being renewed in knowledge in the image of its Creator (Col. 3:10).

We need to give up trying to discipline our old nature and learn to die daily to our fleshly desires. It is a lifelong process of growing in goodness and holiness by focusing on that which is of God and refusing to give in to the old sin nature.

In what ways have you been trying to train your old nature to improve it? Consider how you are able to differentiate between being led by the Spirit or controlled by the flesh.

_____

_____

_____

_____

_____

_____

_____

_____

_____

_____

_____

_____

_____

_____

_____

_____

_____

_____

_____

CARNAL CHRISTIANS

Paul reminds us that some Christians are carnal and some are spiritual. One of the greatest problems in the church today is carnal Christians. If we want to move from being carnal to being spiritual, we must accept as settled that we can *become* spiritual. We need to believe that as many as are led by the Spirit are children of God. We also must acknowledge our carnality if we are to overcome it.

The only way to treat self is have nothing to do with it. This can be done in an instant, but the growth and maturity will be a process that takes many years. The chief mark of a spiritual man is that he has surrendered to the Spirit of God. You now belong to Christ. God will keep and bless you. Stand on the Word of God. God has promised His Holy Spirit to every hungering child. Open your heart and be filled with the Spirit and believe in Christ to bless you.

What are some of the signs of being filled with the Spirit? When you see the word carnal what comes to your mind? Have you taken the step to open your heart and be filled with the Spirit? If not, would you like to do it now?

KNOWING GOD'S WILL

12The best way to know God's will is to be familiar with the Bible. Virtually everything we need to know concerning God's will is in the Bible. David reminds us in Psalm 119:105, "Your word is a lamp to my feet and a light for my path." His word is our guide. The Bible unfolds manifold features of God's will, showing how dynamically it will assist us in life's most practical experiences.

God's Word lights the way for us, giving specific direction for each step. Joshua links the regular application of God's Word to life as the most certain way to success and prosperity. In Joshua 1:8, we read, "Do not let this Book of the Law depart from your mouth; meditate on it day and night, so that you may be careful to do everything written in it. Then you will be prosperous and successful." Let God's Word guide, instruct, teach, and confirm your daily walk and you will go a long way toward living out God's will in your life.

How much of God's Word have you hidden in your heart? What have you found helpful to more effectively hide His Word in your heart? Be careful to do everything that God's Word quickens to your heart.

HUMILITY

No sin is more hateful and abhorrent to God than pride. Pride transforms virtues into vices and blessing into curses. Beauty plus pride equals vanity. Zeal plus pride equals tyranny. Speech plus pride equals criticism. Humility is the antithesis of pride. We must learn to cooperate to the limit with the Holy Spirit by hating our pride and coveting humility.

Matthew 23:12 says, "For whoever exalts himself will be humbled, and whoever humbles himself will be exalted." Humility is the root virtue of the Christian life. When we practice diligent self-examination on a regular basis, humility can be a natural byproduct. According to James, "God opposes the proud but gives grace to the humble" (James 4:6).

Unlearning is often the most important part of learning. We must let go of prejudices, wrong impressions and beliefs that stand in our way to true learning. Our attitude has to be that of humility and willingness to acknowledge our wrong thoughts and develop an eagerness to learn and grow. Humility is the beginning of wisdom. If pride is the greatest sin, then humility must be the greatest virtue.

Can you give examples of some things you had to unlearn? In what areas do you find it easy to fall into pride?

_____

_____

_____

_____

_____

_____

_____

_____

_____

_____

_____

_____

_____

_____

_____

_____

_____

_____

_____

_____

_____

_____

HONEST BEFORE HIM

"Surely, O God, you have worn me out; you have devastated my entire household. You have bound me--and it has become a witness; my gauntness rises up and testifies against me. God assails me and tears me in His anger and gnashes His teeth at me; my opponent fastens on me his piercing eyes. Men open their mouths to jeer at me; they strike my cheek in scorn and unite together against me. God has turned me over to evil men and thrown me into the clutches of the wicked. All was well with me, but He shattered me; He seized me by the neck and crushed me. He has made me His target. . .Again and again He bursts upon me; He rushes at me like a warrior" (Job 16:7-14).

Notice Job's honesty before God. He doesn't seem to have a lot of trouble being honest and reporting his true feelings. It is my contention that, when properly done, journaling will promote honesty in our lives. Why not try it for the next thirty days and see what happens in your life? In what ways do you find it hard to be honest before God?

WE ARE GOD'S MASTERPIECE

We are God's masterpiece. He has created us anew in Christ Jesus, so that we can do the good things He planned for us long ago. It is so important to realize that we are indeed a masterpiece. God knew exactly what He was doing when He made us.

We have so much more ability than we manage to use. It would astound us if we could fully understand how much potential we have, compared to what we use. Man can indeed achieve what his mind can conceive. However, our primary task is to "seek first His kingdom and His righteousness, and all these things will be given to you as well" (Matt. 6:33).

Do you sometimes find yourself questioning God about the way He made you? In that same light are you fully satisfied with your personal design or features? Does the concept that you are a masterpiece designed by God conjure up negative thoughts in your mind?

LOVE DEFINED

"Love is patient, love is kind. It does not envy, it does not boast, it is not proud. It is not rude, it is not self-seeking, it is not easily angered, it keeps no record of wrongs. Love does not delight in evil but rejoices with the truth. It always protects, always trusts, always hopes, always perseveres," (1 Corinthians 13:4-7).

What can I add to one of the most profound passages in all of scripture? This passage is totally a joy to meditate on. Another story of selfless love is presented in 1 Sam.18:3: "Jonathan made a covenant with David because he loved him as himself."

Years ago I learned that love is a deep and abiding concern for the welfare of another at all times. Once I had this clearly in mind I realized that I could obey Jesus' command to love my enemies. Love is a many splendored thing. An entire book could be written on the subject of love, but "God is love" says it all.

Can you write you own definition of love? Are you able to put into writing some of the feelings you sense while reading and meditating on Corinthians 13?

GOD'S TRUE LOVE

"If I speak in the tongues of men and of angels, but have not love, I am only a resounding gong or a clanging cymbal. If I have the gift of prophecy and can fathom all mysteries and all knowledge, and if I have a faith that can move mountains, but have not love, I am nothing. If I give all I possess to the poor and surrender my body to the flames, but have not love, I gain nothing" (1 Corinthians 13:1-3).

This scripture clearly shows that love is the most important gift of all. When we are void of love, none of these acts are worth anything. This certainly deserves our full attention. We know God better through love. According to1 John 4:7, "let us love one another, for love is of God; and everyone who loves is born of God and knows God." The Word of God reminds us in 1 John 4:12, "No one has seen God at any time. If we love one another, God abides in us, and His love has been perfected in us."

Jesus Himself makes it clear by reminding us, "By this all men will know that you are my disciples, if you love one another" (John 13:35).

How have you shown God's love to family members this last week? How would those people with whom you work know that you are a disciple of Christ?

_____

_____

_____

_____

_____

_____

_____

_____

_____

_____

_____

_____

_____

_____

_____

_____

_____

_____

_____

_____

_____

_____

_____

_____

RUNNING THE RACE

Discipline. This means we give up the bad and the good and strive only for the best. There are many ways to fail in the Christian life. But all of them begin with lack of discipline, consciously deciding to take the easy route. We must approach our walk with single-minded determination. Paul says, "This one thing I do!" (Philippians 3:13). The purpose of our discipline is not to do everything by ourselves but it is to learn to draw our strength from Christ.

Determination. "Therefore, since we are surrounded by such a great cloud of witnesses, let us throw off everything that hinders and the sin that so easily entangles, and let us run with perseverance the race marked out for us" (Hebrews 12:1). Watch out for sin that entangles your feet.

Focus on the finish line. We must run to win. Keep an eternal perspective on life. Keep your focus on Christ. Look for the eternal reward. This means forgetting the things behind us, things that would weigh us down. This includes habits and actions that take time and energy.

How can you focus on the finish line and still see where you are running? Can you name some of the weights that are hindrances that you still need to throw off?

_____

_____

_____

_____

_____

_____

_____

_____

_____

_____

_____

_____

_____

_____

_____

_____

_____

_____

_____

_____

_____

_____

_____

_____

ONE LARGE COOPERATIVE ENDEAVOR

In 2 Corinthians 3:18, we read, " And we, who with unveiled faces all reflect the Lord's glory, are being transformed into His likeness with ever-increasing glory. . ."

"Therefore, my dear friends. . .continue to work out your salvation with fear and trembling, for it is God who works in you to will and to act according to his good purpose" (Philippians 2:12-13).

This certainly makes it clear that we are being transformed by the renewing and refreshing of our minds on a daily basis. It requires discipline, but we are not left on our own. God has a wonderful plan for our lives and we need to seek to fulfill it day by day.

To what extent are you aware of God's plan for your life? Can you write it out in a few sentences? Are trying to work out your own salvation without God's help? Or, are you letting Him do it all without you doing your part?

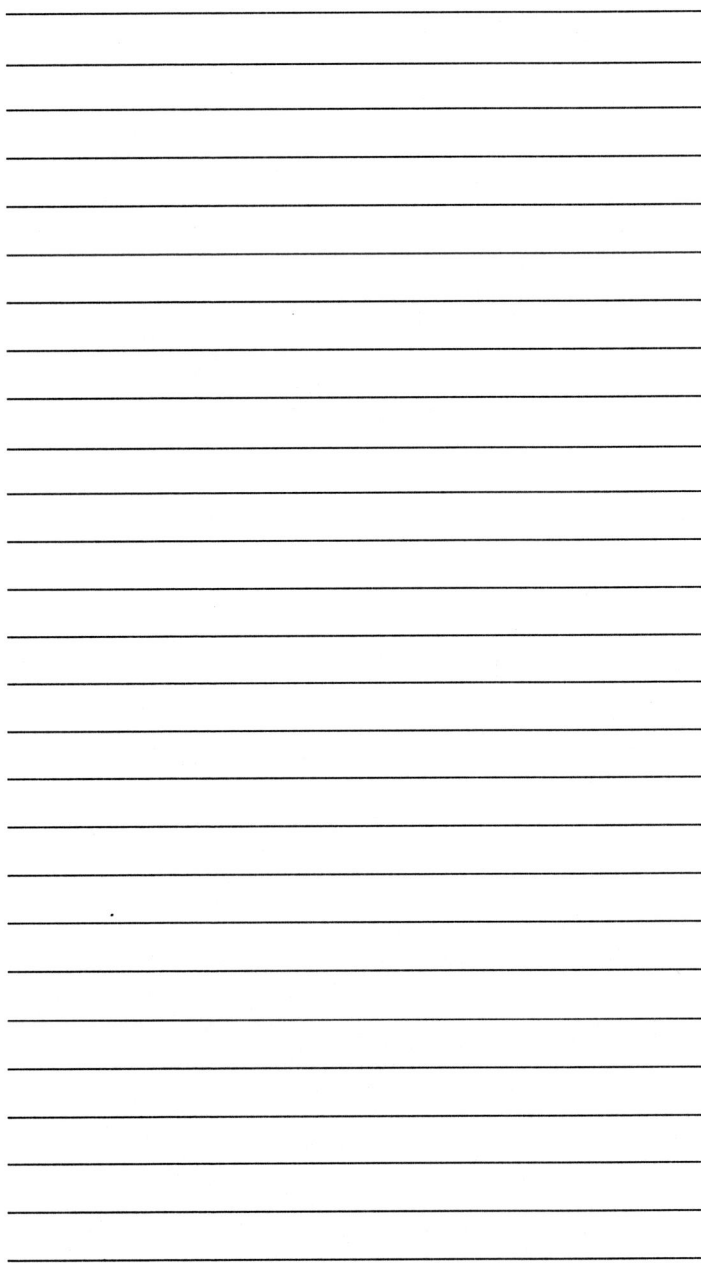

WHERE TO GO FROM HERE

We have heard the case for meditating on the
Word and journaling daily. The real test is where
do you go from here? Were you encouraged and
blessed by learning more of who God is and the
great value of being a man or woman of the Word?
I want to encourage you to try spending time
alone with God for the next 30 days and see what
it does for your life.

Select a book of the Bible and in an organized way
select a quiet place and seek Him by meditating on
a few verses at a time. You choose the Bible translation you wish to use, but the real key is to make
it a daily practice, preferably in the morning, and
to record your personal revelations in a journal.
My Bible and my journal are always with me
every morning. My prayer is that God will bless
you richly as you move out into this wonderful
world of spending time alone with God on a daily
basis.

Printed in the United States
849500002B

9 781928 715290